SOWING, PLANTING, WATERING, AND FEEDING

SOWING, PLANTING, WATERING, AND FEEDING

·Bob Flowerdew·

Skyhorse Publishing

Skyhorse Publishing books may be purchased in bulk at special discounts for sales promotion, corporate gifts, fund-raising, or educational purposes. Special editions can also be created to specifications. For details, contact the Special Sales Department, Skyhorse Publishing, 307 West 36th Street, 11th Floor, New York, NY 10018 or info@skyhorsepublishing.com.

Skyhorse® and Skyhorse Publishing® are registered trademarks of Skyhorse Publishing, Inc.®, a Delaware corporation.

Visit our website at www.skyhorsepublishing.com.

10 9 8 7 6 5 4 3 2 1

Library of Congress Cataloging-in-Publication Data is available on file.

ISBN: 978-1-61608-636-7

Printed in China by 1010 Printing Ltd

Contents

Introduction   6

Sowing   8

Planting   42

Watering   58

Feeding   82

Index   112

Introduction

Gardening involves many things; from mowing the lawn to turning compost, from weeding and pruning to hedge trimming and deadheading. But at the heart of it all lies the nurturing and coaxing of plants we love because we want them to thrive, and, as with babies, their earliest days are the most important. It's crucial to get everything right from the start.

Sowing, planting, watering, and feeding are the four areas in which many mistakes and errors can easily be learned by trial and error. This "learn by your mistakes" approach, although interesting and educational, takes rather long to produce good results. As much as I deplore a too rigid "do it by the book" mentality, at the same time the book is usually right—but only if it's the right book. And for these important subjects there is a "right" way. Here we are dealing with an automatic feedback system—you get it right, then fine; you get it wrong, your results will soon stare you in the face.

Not that these are at all difficult tasks, it's just that some things are better not left to "common sense." For example, it may not, at first, seem very logical that good garden soil should not be used as a sowing medium in a pot for small seeds, or even for growing many plants. But it really is not suitable for a multitude of reasons and so will give disastrous results. Neither is garden soil a good planting medium for containers. Likewise with watering and feeding, counter-intuitively, too much is much, much worse than not enough.

Sowing

We sow seeds to grow plants, or rather so that seedlings will grow on into small plants. Becoming bigger, these eventually flower and set seeds of their own—if we haven't eaten all or part of them before then. Perhaps the majority of seeds sown are for crops, as this is the cheapest way of getting huge numbers of plants. We also commonly sow hardy annuals—tough flowering plants that only live a year or so—as this is almost the only way we can grow them.

Nearly all plants can be grown from seed, especially the wild forms. This is fine for the majority of flowering plants and trees. However some plants produce better results if they are bought in as "choice" plants that have been grafted, slipped, or split, such as most fruit trees and many of the best ornamentals. (These are vegetative methods of multiplying identical plants by growing small pieces of one plant on new roots to maintain unique attributes, such as flower color or, in the case of fruits, to make a smaller tree.) Still, plants grown from seed are usually of a far more vigorous nature than those that have been vegetatively reproduced, are more resistant to pests and diseases, and sometimes are better. This is especially true of the carefully bred F1 varieties, which are very consistent with near identical results but, unfortunately, do not then set seed with the same outcome and thus must be bought fresh each year.

Left: Sow seed as if each was the last left in the world, that is, very thoughtfully and carefully

How seeds work

Seeds are very slow living, but alive nonetheless. They're packages of all the materials, save water and oxygen, needed to make a seedling and to get its first leaves up into the sun. Some seeds stay alive for a very long time, but the vast majority only last a matter of months, or a few years at most, even when stored in cool, dark, and dry conditions.

A few seeds will only germinate when fresh, but most are designed to await the occurrence of certain conditions before germinating. When these do occur, the seeds respond by waking up, sucking in moisture and air, and pushing down roots while raising a seed leaf or two into the light. This germination and emergence is powered by the seed consuming its reserves, using oxygen, which then produces some heat and the seed exudes carbon dioxide and waste substances. (If you have sprouted edible seeds for the table you will have noticed they require regular rinsing to remove this waste matter.)

So seeds need water and oxygen to germinate and grow, and they also need to get rid of carbon dioxide and wastes. Thus, to germinate, most seeds like to be packed around with moist gritty particles—not waterlogged, but moistened and aerated—which then absorb the wastes and help exchange oxygen for carbon dioxide. Once they have started into life, seeds need to push their seed leaves up and out of the growing medium and into the light. The depth that seeds can cope with being planted at varies, but generally the bigger the seed the deeper it may be sown. But be warned, do not bury seeds—too deep is worse than too shallow. The smallest need to be embedded on the surface and the biggest usually not much deeper than a few times their own size.

Right: Sow two seeds in case one fails, and for the squash family, such as these cucumbers, sow on their edge then cover

The effects of temperature and light

Although seeds give off a little heat, usually they respond better if they are kept warm; though not too hot as that soon kills them. Most seeds need a minimum temperature in order to germinate; some need the temperatures to alternate between warmer and cooler. Cold often stops them altogether (although, in some cases, stratification, a period of winter, is needed before seeds will germinate) and any frost kills germinating seed and seedlings much more easily than it does the mature plant.

Not only does cold, wet compost, or soil make it difficult for a seed to make itself warm enough to germinate, but pathogenic bacteria and fungi may successfully attack the seed. While the seed adapts its metabolism from a dormant seed to a seedling its defenses are weak, and if it cannot grow away from the attack, it's lost. Also, bacteria in cold wet soils break down nutrients, which liberates ammonia, probably killing the seedling roots.

Warmer conditions are less dangerous because then growth is more vigorous and the danger period is over sooner.

Seedlings also need plentiful light; if there is not enough of it, emerging seedlings get lanky and drawn, then they yellow and die. Light is essential for photosynthesis and to make the sugars needed for healthy growth; if the conditions are too dim the seedlings waste resources searching for light by growing upwards instead. However, when confined under glass or plastic, the young seedlings cannot handle scorching bright sunlight and are easily killed if the temperature of the soil or air becomes too elevated.

Right: Well spaced seedlings will not waste resources fighting each other

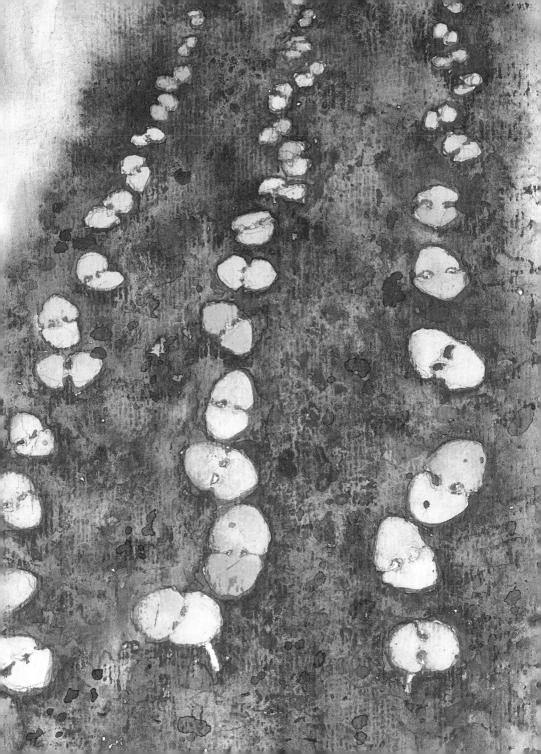

The biggest danger—sowing too many seeds

By far the most common problem is sowing too many seeds too densely. As they grow they compete for resources, choke each other, and become drawn. Intermingled seedlings also become difficult to handle, and then what do you do with so many? Truly, the best approach is to always sow seed sparingly, never to sow more than three times the number of seeds as plants required, and when sowing direct in situ, follow the instructions on the seed packets to guide you as to the spacing between seeds and the depth at which they should be sown.

Left: Sowing tomato seeds three to a pot is better than thirty if all you want are a couple of plants

General seed notes

It is a good idea to read the instructions on the seed packet before you begin sowing, as every seed has different germinating requirements, sometimes even varying with different varieties of one type of plant.

Seed storage—as soon as you get your packets, keep them away from heat, out of the sun, and in a pest-proof airtight box (preferably with a few silica gel bags to absorb any moisture). Keep the box in a cool dark place. Opened packets of seed should be promptly folded shut and put back in the box. If you save your own seed from your plants (NOT from F1 varieties which do not come true), make sure it's well dried and pest free when put away. Large amounts of seeds in their pods, such as peas and beans, are best hung in bags made from net curtains in a cool, dry, rodent-free roof space.

Life span—in near-perfect conditions most seeds keep for a few years. Generally, the bigger seeds stay viable longer than the smallest—and weed seeds better than valued plants! Seed quality and vigor deteriorates over time, so although a percentage of old seeds may germinate in good conditions, they may all fail in tougher ones. (By now any packets with a sow-by date starting 19** are better discarded!)

Testing—if you're not sure about a seed's viability, don't wait to be let down, test it. Sow, say, twenty seeds in a pot of proper sowing compost in a warm place. If twenty come up, it's fine, if fifteen, it's usable, if ten, sow doubled up. If only five come up it doesn't have a chance in the open ground but will be acceptable sown thick in a pot under cover. If less than five, throw the packet away.

Stratifying and vernalizing—are required for some seeds that need a period of cold conditions in order to germinate. Pack the seed in something like sharp sand and overwinter in the open (but protected from pests) to sow the next spring, or refrigerate them, again packed in sand in a box, to simulate winter.

Right: Too many packets, still the wooden trays are handy for keeping them in order

Pre-soaking—once recommended for seeds such as peas and beans, this method may be of use in dry soils in summer but is counterproductive earlier on, especially in cold soils. Seed needs to grow when soil conditions are ready to support it, so fooling it into starting too early is risky.

Chitting—this is a rarely needed method of starting reluctant seeds more quickly. On many seeds the hard seed coat has to degrade before it will let in water; rub through this with sandpaper for earlier germination.

Pre-germination in gel and fluid—a fungicide-free wallpaper paste or similar is used to germinate the seeds, which are then enclosed and protected by it while they are squeezed out into their growing positions. Although some may find this useful, I note it's not widely adopted, even in commercial horticulture, though it offers some advantage for difficult-to-germinate, in situ seed, such as parsnip.

Paper tapes—on the market again are paper tapes and sheets that have the seed ready spaced on them. The tape, disc, or square is laid on leveled compost or soil when you want to sow. The compost or soil must be uniformly moist for this method to work, but it is a labor saver, though has never proved widely popular.

Laying seed on edge—seeds have preferred alignments for germination and it's claimed that flat ones, such as cucurbits, do better laid on edge rather than flat. I find little difference; but to be sure I sow three—one flat, one on edge, and one vertically.

"Seed" potatoes or "sets" chitted into earlier growth in a light, frost-free place

The benefit of sowing under cover

If you sow indoors or under cover you can start seeds earlier in the year, even without extra heat—they just need the warmth that is trapped under glass or plastic. This means we can grow plants that need more time to flower or crop than our brief summers allow.

We can sow indoors when the weather and/or soil are not suitable. And we can do so in comfort! However, this usually means sowing into some sort of pot or tray. (Yogurt cartons, and the like, are acceptable if they are given drainage holes.) Individual pots, preferably plastic and clean, are useful for seeds that make big plants fairly rapidly, such as the cucumber and zucchini family, and those that resent disturbance. Frequently, though, many seeds are sown in a small pot then pricked out or separated once they have emerged with their first leaves into individual pots, or trays, of richer compost. Multi-celled plastic trays are much used for bedding plants and hardy crops such as onions and beetroot. It's vitally important when using these to move the plants on promptly, as each cell has such a tiny volume of compost. Trays—flat open ones and plastic now, no longer wood—are ideal for bulk sowings that can be separated out before they get too big, such as onions, salads, and bedding plants. Deeper is better, but otherwise root-directing containers and special pots with extra air holes are possibly useful for growing certain plants, but not really much benefit for sowing seeds. (Citrus and other plants that require most soil aeration and drainage in order to grow well may find extra air holes useful.) I must repeat an earlier warning here: do not sow too many seeds together as they will compete for nutrients, water, and light. If you want a half dozen plants then sowing a dozen seeds will supply more than enough, so why sow more only to have to discard most of them? If you want to be sure of the best seedlings, sow three small batches a few days or a week apart; nearly always one batch will be much the best and more vigorous. Often, later-sown batches outperform earlier ones (most probably because the weather is getting warmer).

Right: These corn and bean plants (good companions) will crop under cover many weeks before the outdoor plants

Preparing to sow seeds

Drainage is crucial; if sowing compost cannot drain it drowns most seeds, which, if you remember, need oxygen and they cannot get this in waterlogged soil. So there must be drainage holes in all sowing containers, although, even so, they're seldom big or numerous enough. To stop compost washing out, fill the bottom of each pot with coarse material, such as grit or gravel or pieces of broken pot. Standing pots in saucers of water dooms seeds to waterlogging.

Using the right composts for sowing seeds is crucial; it must be proper, fresh, store-bought, specific sowing compost to give the best results. Multi- or general-purpose, potting, planting, or homemade composts will not serve well for any but the most robust seeds. You cannot do better, reliably, than use the John Innes formula sowing compost—this consists of a mix of loam (rotted grass turves), peat, grit, and sharp sand and has low levels of nutrients. Seeds have all the fertility they need and are handicapped by fertilizers in their sowing compost. Once the seedlings have emerged they can be moved to a pot with a richer diet. For a very few seeds, especially very small ones such as fuchsias and begonias, you may need to sow onto fine grit, vermiculite or perlite, leaf mold, or even peat, instead of compost. Indeed, ericaceous (acid lovers) obviously need an acid compost. But for the majority of common seeds the JI formula is well suited. It's not a brand, but a formula, so it varies with the manufacturer; choose a big name, look for a quick-moving pile, not soaking wet bags, at a reputable supplier and buy fresh stock, not old. Store bags in the cool and dry and bring them out into the warm a day or three before using to warm up the compost for sowing.

Right: An economical bottom layer of well drained, but seed-ridden, soil-based compost is covered with a top layer of proper store-bought (sifted) John Innes sowing compost

Place coarse bits in bottom to aid drainage

Fill over brim with sifted sowing compost and wipe off excess

Sow seeds sparingly and separately

Push seeds to suitable depth firmly

Cover seeds with sifted compost

Pat firmly

DO NOT FORGET THE LABEL

Soak from bottom up for half an hour
THEN DRAIN!

I sift my sowing compost immediately before use with a coarse sifter. This is not to remove much, but to give it uniformity by reducing lumps and, more importantly, to reintroduce air that has long been squeezed out. Do not sift out anything but the odd coarse chunky piece, as too fine a compost is not wanted; somewhat gritty is usually better.

I repeat: do not try to use anything other than specific sowing compost for germinating seeds in containers, and preferably use the John Innes formula. If you must try something else, compare it side by side with JI. Having said all that, I must confess I occasionally fiddle with JI sowing compost. I add small amounts of crushed charcoal, leaf mold, or lime, as these seem to help germinate some difficult seeds. The charcoal is good for slow-germinating seeds as it keeps compost sweeter; use leaf mold for acid and woodland plants (it has special residues and microorganisms) and lime for brassicas and other lime lovers. However, such fiddling is risky; remember the JI formula was methodically arrived at and has proved efficacious for more than half a century.

Fast-growing seeds, say marrows, even when sown individually in pots or cells, run out of nutrients fairly quickly. They could have liquid feeds when watering or, alternatively, you could fill the lower half of the pot with proper potting compost and then top up with proper sowing compost (this is known as double layering). This way the seed is surrounded by the right medium and once growing gets under way the seedling will find the richer stuff underneath.

Take care when sowing seed to get the position in the compost just right; too shallow and seed may dry out or have insufficient weight to push against, too deep it may not germinate and even if it did it could never emerge. So, first read the packet, then, depending on the instructions, place the seed on the surface of the compost, or in holes or drills (long, narrow, shallow holes) at whatever depth is required. Be careful to get this right, including the depth of the layer of covering material in your calculations. Remember, seed needs to be in intimate contact with sowing compost, so gently but determinedly firm down the covering material with something flat—a wood block is good.

Some seeds need a flash of light to start germination (farmers plowing at night have less weedy fields—honestly!) and if they are deeply buried in the dark they may remain dormant. A very few, usually tiny, seeds may need to be in the light to germinate, which means they should be sown on the surface of the soil and not covered. A sheet of glass may be placed on top, but this can cook the seeds in bright sun, so a sheet of white paper is safer, and does not drip any condensation that builds up. Some seed may need to be in the dark for the first days until germinated but then needs uncovering immediately—again, read the instructions on the packet!

You cannot sensibly use a sowing compost when wet and muddy, or when powder dry. If you need to get it back to a decent moistness such stuff would be better replaced by a fresh batch. Your seeds are too precious to give them anything second rate. So, having sown seeds in slightly moist compost, firm it down then stand your pots, or whatever, in a tray of warm water until the surface darkens with moisture, then drain off immediately. This is far better than pouring water on top, which packs compost down, expelling air.

Sift out only the coarsest bits but do sift to reintroduce air

Mix fine or sticky seed with ground lime or wood ash to make it visible and easier to sow

Caring for seedlings

Watch out for damping off: nasty fungal diseases, and occasionally bacterial ones, attack seedlings so that they emerge one day only to wither the next. Using proper, fresh, store-bought sowing compost and clean water will prevent this from happening. Although bigger plants generally prefer rainwater, it's sensible to only use warm tap water for seeds and seedlings. Various "antiseptics" have been used to prevent damping off, but these may also hinder germination themselves so are probably best avoided.

Left: Sweet pea seedlings will soon need moving on to bigger pots from these small cells—and what has happened to the seedling in the bottom right hand corner... umm

The right conditions

Sowing with extra warmth makes it possible to grow all sorts of tender, half-hardy, and long-season plants. And growing with some warmth makes other sowings come up faster and more surely. All you need is a warm radiator by a bright window and a clear plastic bag; an airing cupboard is good if checked every day, but as soon as you see a shoot, the pot, in its clear plastic bag, needs moving to a warm, light windowsill.

A proper propagator is usually electrically warmed and has a clear plastic cover to keep the heat and humidity in. It will enable you to grow most plants from seed, but as the seedlings grow they quickly fill it. So ideally you need another propagator, perhaps not quite as warm, to move the young plants to. You can buy electric warming mats to stand them on and make plastic covers to go over.

A cold frame in a greenhouse is a halfway house between a small propagator and an unheated greenhouse. It is incredibly useful, especially if equipped with a little warmth, and can house plants until they're safe to move to the staging. One can also grow melons in them in summer and use them to house tender plants through winter.

A common error is not ventilating propagators or seed trays or pots with glass sheets laid on them. Not only does the compost cook under glass in bright sun, but the air gets stale too. Remember, seeds are breathing as they germinate and it's not until they have green leaves in the light that they can photosynthesize and use the energy from light to make food for themselves, consuming the carbon dioxide. Whenever it is warm enough, open propagators to let out stale air, and try to do this at least twice a day.

A position that is too warm and too dim is a common problem that results in lanky, soft, drawn, and yellow seedlings. Giving extra heat starts off seed well but the seedlings soon need it cooler—though not cold! Make sure all glass, plastic, and so on, is clean enough to let in as much natural light as possible, and consider purchasing a special growing light if your propagator or greenhouse sits in a naturally shady place.

When you move a seedling from a warm propagator to a cooler windowsill, outdoors, or onto the staging in an unheated greenhouse, it must adjust to the new, tougher conditions. This is a process known as hardening off. Help it to adjust by not potting it up at the same time as moving it, by being careful to water sparingly and with warm water, and to keep out draughts by covering with a clear plastic bag or similar. If cold nights are likely, place plastic bottles of hot water among the plants and cover them over with sheets of newspaper. But no amount of hardening off helps a tender plant resist frost or severe cold, so never move any plants to colder conditions until all risk of frost has passed or without cosseting them with extra protection for the first week or so.

Young pepper plants are easily chilled or drowned and safer in this propagator

Pricking out and potting on

Once the seeds have germinated and emerged from the soil, they start to compete with each other. A proper sowing compost has little fertility so seedlings are soon hungry; now they must be transplanted, or pricked out, and given their own pot, cell, or place in a tray of richer compost. The very tiniest and most delicate seedlings may be pricked out into more sowing compost rather than risk overwhelming them, but generally richer potting compost is required. Handle the seedlings by a leaf, not by holding the more easily damaged stem, tease the roots out with a pencil tip, or similar, and replant them firmly into their new home.

Once the seedlings have reached a certain size their pots or cells become confining and restrict their growth, so they need moving on or potting on into bigger pots of potting or multi-purpose compost, especially if they are not to be planted outside until later. A check caused by sitting in too small a pot not only stunts growth, but the tiny amount of compost they are in will dry out rapidly. In this situation it will require more water and more frequent watering to prevent the plant suffering drought stress and any further damage.

So, half-fill the new pot loosely and, holding the seedling by a leaf, lower the roots onto the compost of the new pot. Add a little more compost to the pot to cover the roots, then firm down gently but deliberately using your fingers. (Roots will never be damaged by such pressure, though without care a tiny stem may be.) Stand the pot in warm water to moisten the compost, then remove and allow it to drain.

Once a seedling is growing away it may need support. I find twiggy sticks cut from the garden better than smooth canes for supporting most small plants—never reuse old ones as they can carry diseases and pests. If you must tie up to a cane, then do so around a leaf or flower stalk, not the stem, until the plant is much bigger and sturdier.

Two seedlings to a cell is acceptable

These marigolds are congested and
must be divided up and potted

It's easiest to divide rootballs when they're soaking in water

Lower the seedling in and position its roots

Firm the compost around the potted marigold seedling

Add sifted compost up to the brim

Sowing outdoors in the ground

Although more natural, this is also more risky. Our seed is at the behest of the weather and is prey to all sorts of pests and diseases that are not usually found under cover. The soil needs to have warmed up, be friable and in good tilth (like bagged sowing compost in texture), moist, and after sowing several measures must be taken against various ills, including weeds and birds. However, seed sown in situ does usually make better plants than those planted out from seed sown in pots, and once sown, seed in the ground requires much less attention—especially if a good seed bed was made with nicely worked gritty soil or, even better, one topped with proper sowing compost.

There is absolutely no sense in sowing seed outdoors out of season. Under cover you might get away with it, but check the instructions on the packet before sowing. On average you can sow hardy annuals and tougher vegetables outdoors from early spring, the bulk of outdoor sowings in mid-spring, and tender but faster growing vegetable, such as squashes, once the last frost has passed in late spring come early summer.

Sow the seeds in suitable soil; there's little point sowing the seed of acid-loving plants in limey soil, or alkaline-lovers in acidic soils. Plants that thrive on light, dry, sandy soil will likely not even germinate in cold wet clay. Although you can choose a better sowing compost, it's hard to alter your soil by much. It's often a good idea to ask local gardeners which varieties of what do well in your area, as these are the best ones to start with.

Although the weather usually provides moist soil in spring, it's best to water drills and let it soak in before sowing. Warm water gives a slight benefit as it soaks in better and marginally improves the temperature. Seaweed solution may be added, well diluted, to discourage pests and diseases, but liquid feed or fertilizers should not be given until the plants have got going. Do not water seeds again until the seedlings have emerged or you may cause capping (see page 41). However, once seedlings are growing, water diligently if no rain falls for several days, as while seedlings are small their roots are not deep. In windy springs the soil quickly dries out, checking the growth of seedlings, so water them before they show they need it, preferably with clean water and without splashing, which can infect the seedlings with disease.

Pre-warming the soil makes quicker and more successful germination; you can cover the soil with black plastic sheeting or fix a clear sheet just above it. Or you can use a cold frame, cloche, or plastic tunnel; just put it in place two weeks or so before sowing.

As with sowing in pots, when sowing outdoors be careful to get the depth right according to which seed you are using. In heavier, wet soils, sow slightly shallower; in light, dry soils, sow slightly on the deeper side. Some use a hoe to draw out a drill to sow into; I rake the soil level and press a broom handle or cane into the tilth to make the drill, carefully water this, then sow, cover, and firm.

Although it's normal to use soil to cover the seed, this ensures weeds mix in with the emerging seedlings. It's often worth filling the drill and covering seeds with sifted proper sowing compost. This also marks the sites of the seeds and ensures more accurate weeding until the seedlings emerge.

Just as when sowing seed in pots, it's essential to firm seed into the soil but not to press the soil into a muddy brick. Gentle pressing with the back of a rake is sufficient. Insufficient firming often results in poor shows.

For many seeds you may wish to put a cloche, or individual plastic bottle cloche or plastic sheet over for extra warmth and weather protection. A cloche will not keep off hard frost but may deflect light ones or at least reduce the effects. It may also keep off some pests.

Also ensure some anti-capping measures; many soils tend to cap or crust where the topmost layer above the seed turns into a solid cake. This annoyingly stops single seedlings emerging while those sown too thickly may lift the crust off in pieces. Keeping the rain off after sowing is effective at preventing a crust forming; alternatively, use sowing compost as the drill fill as this is designed not to cap. Another approach is to carefully rake the crust or cap a day or two before the seedlings emerge. (Say carrots are sown, these take about two weeks to emerge; so on about day twelve it's safe to gently rake over, and a day or three later they'll appear.)

As with anti-capping, you can time weeding to avoid damaging new seedlings. So on day twelve of the carrot example you pass a hobby blow torch, hot air, or steam gun rapidly over weed seedlings in the bed. They wither and die and a few days later your carrots emerge, weed-free. Using drill fills of sowing compost also keeps weeds away from seedlings, and mulches in between seedlings suppress most weeds. Otherwise, hoe or hand-weed as the seedlings must not have competition. At the same time, thin emerged seedlings to a fair spacing. You may even transplant some to fill gaps. Even root vegetables can be successfully moved when tiny. Do not ignore thinning, as seedlings too close together makes for poor crops and displays of bloom. Slightly too few plants always do far better than slightly too many.

Put in place anti-pest measures early on—there is little point sowing, say, beets, if you know birds will razor off the seedlings. Plastic bottle cloches, wire netting, guards made of old wire baskets, glitter bangs, and such tricks should be employed before a known problem reoccurs. Fine mesh netting on sticks, well fastened down at the edges is particularly useful against pests such as carrot root fly and brassica butterflies.

Left: Cloches can be bought or made from large plastic bottles

Planting

One can garden for years without ever sowing anything. Indeed, the novice may do well to avoid sowing seeds for their first few seasons. However, you're still likely to plant. This is speedier and more certain, as you're not dealing with vulnerable seedlings but with larger, tougher plants already well on their way to flowers or crops.

Garden stores and mail order suppliers now offer an expanding range of crop plants, bedding plants and the like, as tiny plugs or starters. These are best potted up and kept under cover initially, then hardened off and planted out. Using these almost always ensures good results, as the worst weather and soil conditions are avoided. However, they're more expensive than seeds and the range is not as wide, though it is sufficient for

Right: Top left: Mail order strawberry plants. **Top right:** Carefully positioned plant in pot filled with potting compost over drainage. **Bottom left:** Filling up with sifted potting compost. **Bottom right:** Potted plants soaking for half an hour THEN DRAINING!

You can also plant out much larger specimens, almost full-grown even, from larger pots. These make an almost instant display in some cases and are usually very reliable. Given the right aftercare and watering, most can be planted any time of the year, though autumn and spring are generally better. In autumn and early winter you can buy bare-rooted trees and shrubs; these are dug from the ground, transplant well while "dormant," and may be quite large. Indeed, even huge trees can be transplanted, though the effort and cost involved are more than proportional.

Bedding plants for summer displays and most crops are planted through mid and late spring, the tender ones, such as tomatoes, after the last frosts in earliest summer. Herbaceous plants (those with no woody parts permanently above ground) are planted in autumn before the soil chills or in early spring before growth resumes. Bare-rooted trees and shrubs are best planted in autumn and are not as happy with spring planting. Evergreens and tender plants may be better planted in late spring, then in a hard winter the nursery bears the loss, not you.

If plants have been raised under cover and you put them straight out into the cold soil and cold winds they will get checked, if not killed outright. So they need hardening off, or acclimatizing to the new, colder outdoor temperatures. Put them in a sheltered sunny spot during the day each day and bring them in at night, and do this for up to a week before planting out. Even so, it does help to plant into pre-warmed soil and to provide a cloche, cold frame, or at least netting protection in the windiest and coldest weather and for frosty nights.

For larger subjects it's often worth making their planting holes in the soil some time before you plant, so that air and warmth can penetrate. It's foolish to force plants into too small holes. Bigger is always better, wider is better than deeper, and breaking up the soil into a fine tilth, moist but not wet, helps the roots establish. If your holes fill with water, make them deeper, wider, break up the bottom, and do not plant until they drain. Or plant on slight mounds of soil.

It is usually necessary to improve soil before planting, but it's now thought not a good plan to mix manures, fertilizers, or whatever into planting holes as the roots may then be reluctant to leave that spot. It is considered better to apply these earlier before planting and to make sure they are well incorporated overall, or to apply them later as mulches or top dressings that are raked in the year after planting, when the roots have grown ready for richer food. However, adding grit or sharp sand to heavy clay soils, and clay to light sandy soils is sensible as these improve the soil texture without affecting the nutrient status by much.

With all store-bought plants, and gifts, inspect them thoroughly for obvious pests and diseases, such as scale insects, aphids, and bugs, before planting them in your garden. Pot-grown plants should be knocked out of their containers and the roots searched diligently for signs of such woes as vine weevil grubs. Some enthusiasts with plant collections, especially of rare or expensive species, keep all new plants in a separate area for a month or so in order that hidden problems are spotted before they infect or infest the rest.

Once planted, you can often get away with walking away, but regular watering for the next growing season seriously improves results. Protection from the weather early on in spring is sensible, as big and well-established plants resist better than freshly planted ones. The

first year dead—or even live—heading and de-fruiting to prevent energy being diverted from establishing is always worthwhile. Feeding, either liquid, foliar, or top dressing, is probably not needed in the first year, except for hungry annual crops such as corn. Mulches benefit most plants except the prostrate varieties. Weeding is essential as weeds seriously compete with the new plants.

Something to watch for during hard frosts is frost heave—when the soil loosens up when the water within it expands as ice. Anything planted in autumn can be lifted up and almost out of its planting hole. As the soil defrosts, go round and tread the roots and soil firm again. (Never, ever plant into cold holes with frozen soil, as the ice may then persist for many weeks.)

Right: Planted under plastic, plants need more attention to watering

Soft, small, and herbaceous plants

Pot-grown plants, once hardened off, should be well watered the day before planting. Ideally, the planting holes are made, watered, and allowed to drain before planting, rather than trying to add water later. The plants should be knocked out of their pots and planted immediately so that light and air do not damage the roots. The hole should be adjusted to the correct depth by adding soil so the plant will stand at the same level with the ground as when the plant was in the pot. Once the rootball is inserted and the surrounding soil firmed around its roots, then nip a bit of leaf and pull—if the leaf does not tear but the plant heaves out, it was not firmly enough set!

With small and soft plants with a freshly grown rootball, the whole lot can be planted untouched. However, if the plant has been potted for some time, it's better to tease out some of the roots so the ball does not bind itself. The bigger the final subject, the more the rootball needs teasing. For

Don't just dig out the soil but break it up fine at the same time

Make the hole much bigger than needed

Fill with water and let it drain away before planting, preferably a whole day before

those that need most teasing apart, agitate and break up the ball in water, then plant it with the roots spread out in their respective directions (as for bare-rooted, see page 48).

If transplanting from seed or nursery beds, dig up the plants carefully, retaining as big a rootball as possible, then plant immediately as if from pots. Do not dunk the roots in mud or fill the holes with mud, as some people foolishly suggest. Coating the roots with mud may help them survive a journey, but being planted in mud means it dries and shrinks, leaving gaps and cracks that harm the roots. But worse, mud has no air, and remember roots need oxygen to grow, so mud is almost the worst thing you can surround them with. Large air gaps are *the* worst though, so plant firmly ensuring soil is well packed all round the rootball by jiggling the ball as you feed in friable soil. If in doubt, start again. (Small holes are far more difficult to fill well than larger ones as the small gap prevents the soil reaching round all parts.)

Some plants, especially brassicas, are lifted twice, a method known as double lifting. The first time this is done to break their tap roots, before they are immediately replanted, usually in the

Plantlets are more easily teased from others after a thorough soaking of the root-mat

Place each plantlet in a pre-watered hole, fix root-ball firmly with moist soil and/or compost

same position. They then grow a more fibrous rootball and then when eventually transplanted to their final position do so more assuredly than if they had not been lifted previously.

The major difference with bare-rooted planting is that instead of popping in a lump of compost with the roots held in place, you have to position each of the roots and infill them with soil, firming as you go. Thus, holding the plant with one hand, position the lowermost roots and trickle soil about them, jiggling the plant to intersperse it among them, then press this firm. Then you position the next tier of roots and intersperse them with soil in the same way and firm down the soil (you can tread it down gently as the roots will not be harmed by such pressure). Finally, deal with those roots just under the surface similarly. Hopefully, if you get it right, the crown or base of the stem is now at ground level, not buried more deeply or more exposed than when in the ground previously. On some plants you can see a difference in coloration on the stem marking the original level.

Herbaceous plants and a few suckering, thicket-forming shrubs can be divided on planting. Carefully cut through the crowns (try washing the soil away first) and leave good buds on each piece. You can multiply the plants into several more and, conveniently, most plants look better as groups of three, five, or seven rather than as one big clump.

Fill the rest of the hole above the rootball with surrounding soil, ideally mixed with compost

Press firmly and level—or make slightly bowl shaped to catch water

Place weather and pest protection immediately

Apply a generous mulch of weed-free material around almost all newly planted subjects, except warmth-loving vegetables such as corn, melons, and prostrate growers such as thymes. Mulch keeps the roots warmer in winter, cooler in summer, and moister in dry conditions, so promoting their more rapid establishment.

As when sowing, it's not sensible to plant already knowing the poor things will likely be taken by slugs, rabbits, or whatever plagues your garden. Protect your plants by taking precautions; from netting, fleeces, and cloches to slug pubs, bird scarers, and man traps. (Oops, sorry, the latter are illegal in the United States; better install CCTV here so you can watch them rob you...)

Once planted, as with seeds, it's not good to water immediately after planting, and it is much better done before. However, start watering soon and keep watering for the first growing season, as little else makes so much difference to growth.

Press plastic cylinder into ground—be careful not to go through roots

A simple cylinder cut from a plastic bottle stops slugs and crawling pests, makes a warm microclimate and yet allows quick and most effective watering

Bulbs, corms, and rhizomes

Doubtless you will plant some bulbs, rhizomes, and corms; if so, only select firm wholesome-looking ones, as any defect may import a disease. Be careful not to damage the basal plate of such bulbs as onion

sets, which some may foolishly push into the ground. A damaged plate may rot even if it manages to still root. Make holes first with a dibber or trowel, plant the bulb, and cover it with soil, pressing down firmly. Following the same plan as for seed drills, of filling them with sterile, weed-free compost instead of soil, is sensible for valuable plants as then no weeds appear close by. Mulching also helps. As does getting them the right way up...

Planting at the right depth is crucial for bulbs and sets. The same rules apply as for seeds; generally, in heavy soils, plant shallower and in light soils, deeper—but first read the instructions. It's usually from the top that you measure; such that, a 1 inch bulb, planted 2 inches deep, needs a 3-inch hole. For such bulbs as shallots and onion sets, where you want the bulb to sit on the soil surface, position each and hold it in place with a small pile of soil, sand, or, preferably, weed-free potting compost. Once the roots have established this pile can be brushed away.

When planting valuable bulbs in heavy clay soils, make the hole deeper, fill the bottom with sharp sand, add the bulb, then add more sharp sand, embalming it in a slug-resistant, well-draining envelope.

Most herbaceous plants generally leave some evidence of their crowns when they die back in winter, but bulbs may disappear without trace. Thus marking their positions with labels, a dressing of gravel or sharp sand, or copper rings (also used to keep away slugs) will stop accidental damage when nothing shows above ground. Of course, if you cover them with a cloche or a plastic bottle, other markings are not needed. Where squirrels, mice, and so on are a problem—filching bulbs—you may also need traps and barriers.

Left: Onions must be grown precisely on the surface of the bed or they get thick necks and store badly
Right: Starting off onion sets early in multi-celled trays enables the planting of only the best, and each with a rootball that fixes them neatly in place

Trees and shrubs

The major difference when planting these is the matter of scale. More care needs to be taken with firming in trees and to support them, because the wind will rock them, loosening the roots and even killing them occasionally. Weed control is always important, even for trees, and those planted into lawns or meadow need the area of turf removed underneath them to be as large as possible. If planting against a garden wall, do not let the branches rub or touch it as then there is no room for them to expand, and make the plant's trunk stand a hand's width away from the wall at least. (Some fear subsidence when trees are grown near houses, but small shrubs and trees on dwarfing stock are rarely troublesome.)

Trees and big shrubs need watering for longer after planting than smaller subjects, simply because of their size. And it's important to plant at the same depth they are used to; with large deep holes this may be difficult to judge, so lay a straight cane over the hole to get the level right. Adjust the depth so the cane is at the same height with any soil mark on the tree's trunk that shows where it was potted or planted up to before.

Some believe, and this may well be true, that trees and shrubs should not only be planted at the same depth they're used to but with the same orientation to the sun. This is possible with your own plants but not so easy with store-bought stock. (And be warned, moss and algae grow on the damp side not, as often claimed, the north side.)

Stakes are necessary to support trees in the first year to stop the roots moving, but these can be very short, just ankle height out of the ground will do. However, grafted trees, especially those with a weak graft on dwarfing stock, need taller stakes to prevent the head breaking the trunk off where it's grafted. A classic mistake is to plant the tree then break several branches while hammering a stake through the roots, damaging several on the way. Instead, position the tree, put the stake in a suitable place, remove the tree from the hole, drive in the stake, offer back the tree, and tie it loosely to the stake. Place the cane across the hole, adjust the

Left: A pad of old carpet and a nylon stocking acceptably secure
this sapling to a short stake, preventing the roots rocking

tree's position to get the depth right, then fill in and firm around the roots, deepest first and placing each higher root in place as you fill. Finally, check the depth again, firm around the roots, and adjust the ties, tightening them. Use a proper tree tie, a good, wide, soft belt of nylon stockings, or a bicycle tube, but never, ever use thin wire or plastic string as these cut into the trunk. Do not forget the compressible rubber block that goes in between the trunk and the stake, this acts as a cushion so the tie can be tight without constricting.

Don't forget the label!

Old books often advocated cutting back trees and shrubs hard when planting; however my research suggests they had both richer soil (more horse muck about) and thus better, more vigorous plants that they could cut back hard when planting. If you need to rework the top of the plant, it's probably better to cut it back hard the year after planting, as then you will have stronger regrowth with less risk of total loss, but if you move something while in leaf, it may help to trim it a little.

When moving small shrubs from pots and containers, treat them much as other plants. Unless they are already root-bound they do not need much teasing out. For trees, especially large-growing species, it's best to tease out all the roots as for bigger and tougher plants. This means you can only plant trees well from autumn until possibly earliest spring, as doing this in growth would check them too much. Not teasing out is too risky; planting a tree that will reach house height with its first yards of roots curled in a tight ball is foolish.

When you have grown your own, try to move plants from nursery beds with whole rootballs with soil attached, if possible. Dig a trench around each plant, then cut underneath and, ideally, drag a plastic sheet under to help lift it out in one. Gently move the plant to a new site, planting it immediately.

Bare-rooted is how most trees and bigger shrubs are supplied by mail order nurseries and garden stores in autumn and early winter. You generally get much bigger specimens this way than if they were pot-grown, but they're often damaged, despite careful packing and handling. On arrival, immediately unpack, check you got what you ordered, ensure dried-out roots are soaked for a half hour and no more, then temporarily pot up and store the plant in a sheltered corner if you can't plant it out immediately. Any damaged roots should be snipped off where feasible, likewise damaged branches. With valuable trees, cauterize wounds with a flame and seal with a pruning compound, especially with stone fruits (Prunus genus) as these suffer a disease, silver leaf, which gets into wounds at any time other than midsummer.

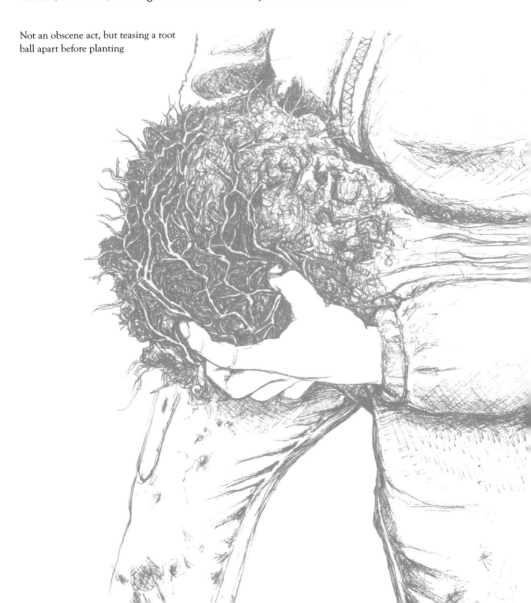

Not an obscene act, but teasing a root ball apart before planting

Watering

It would be strange being a gardener and not watering. It is one of the attributes of a gardener, and enables us to make the biggest difference. We give water to favored plants and they prosper, giving us bigger crops, lusher foliage, and better flowers. Even in the wettest counties there are periods when natural rainfall is insufficient; most crops need an inch per week during the growing season. Under cover our plants totally rely on us for all their water and without us they perish.

Such an apparently simple exercise does, however, have many facets and there are ways in which one can water more efficiently and, more importantly, more effectively.

Right: Watering with the rose, spraying the water upwards, and then down in little arcs, does less damage than with the rose set like a shower head

Why water?

The building block, well, nine-tenths approximately, of every living thing is water. Water is used to make every cell and its components and then to fill and surround them with more water and water-based materials. If you dry plant material you're left with much less; most of the weight has gone. Just think of dried herbs: if you then bake them you break down and drive off even more water until you are left with a minute amount of charred black material, mostly carbon. If this is burned, the microscopic bit of ash remaining is the minerals. So if you want lush foliage, plenty of flowers, and fat, succulent crops, you need to make sure your plants never run short of water.

Plants breathe and transpire water and oxygen when sunlight reaches their leaves (or other green bits); by giving out water they create a form of suction with their sap, which in turn sucks in water from around their roots. (This is because as the sap gets thicker, by giving off water from the leaves, it tries to dilute itself by sucking in more.) However, most plants can absorb water through their leaves as well, indeed we foliar feed plants by spraying them with water and fertilizer. Plants also excrete solvents to aid their roots in penetrating the soil, and at times of high humidity many plants exude water from the edges of their leaves (known as guttation).

But the main consumption of water is for transpiration—and it's not small; trees give off hundreds of gallons of water every day, and even a humble tomato plant loses gallons every week. And, of course, the heaviest loss is when the sun is strong and photosynthesis is taking place, making carbohydrates from carbon dioxide and water, so then water is needed both for transpiration and as a building block.

Water is also the solvent that provides transport for all the various materials transferring in and out of the plant. The inflow of soil water into the sap brings in nutrients and carries them to all parts of the plant, and at the same time this water carries sugars down from the leaves to the feed processes elsewhere within the plant. The sap is akin to blood and must not get too thick or too thin and plants have developed their own way of controlling this; in winter when it's freezing, no water can be extracted from the soil, and so deciduous plants drop their leaves so

they do not lose water they can't replace. Evergreens use little water when it is cold, however if freezing conditions persist for long, and worse with harsh winds, then evergreens become desiccated: their leaves brown and softer shoots die back.

If plants are short of water at their roots and the air around their foliage is moist they find it difficult to transpire (just like we need to sweat more when the conditions are hot and humid than when the air is hot and dry), and it's then that fungus diseases, such as mildews and rust, get in. These diseases need the leaf surfaces to be wet to "germinate," so it's very bad to lightly sprinkle plants with water in dry soil as this can initiate the diseases; far better is to soak the plants' roots without making the air or leaves moist.

If you want bigger crops and lusher flowers, water. The simple reason why we water is that when we do so generously we are generously rewarded. Watering works!

Above: Water seed and seedlings by standing in trays of water, half an hour and no more, then draining!

When to water

We should sensibly water when the plants need it. Outdoors this is unlikely to be from the end of summer until the start of spring, when plants growing in open ground need about 1 inch of rain per week. Even in wetter states there may be a week or more of dry weather, and it's most urgent to water plants that are small seedlings, as yet unequipped with deep root systems to find their own water. It's rarely possible to over-water outdoors in the open ground during the growing season. Conversely, under cover we may need to give water to plants in the depth of winter to stop them desiccating, yet they're barely able to grow in the low light. This is when judging watering is hardest: it's far easier to kill plants in pots under cover by over-watering in winter than by under-watering.

Of course, the plants' needs for water change, with little being needed when it is small, more as it grows, and much more in the rush of spring. Then at maturity the demand drops again.

And, of course, each day's needs depend on the strength of the sun and the dryness of the air, as well as the stage of growth. And every plant is different.

As well as the variation from summer to winter and day-to-day under cover, there's also controversy as to what time of day to water. Personally, I reckon it's best to water in the morning, as the plants are cold from the night so the water will warm up with them and be available when they need it during the day. Others maintain it's better to water at the end of each day; however, then the plants are chilled by the watering and go into the night with damp about them, which I suspect is not good. But ultimately the best time to water is whenever you can, and more often than not that will not always be the same time of day anyway.

It's good to get into a watering routine; there's little benefit in giving huge amounts one week, then little another. Plants become used to your regime; if you keep it constant they adjust as best they can—vary it and they're lost. Worst of all is leaving it until the compost or soil dries out, then the water does not wet the soil but runs straight through it. Adding a drop of dishwashing liquid or soap helps wet the soil by breaking the surface tension and using warm water is quicker for the soil to absorb than cold (and more comfortable for the plants). Big plants in small pots of compost may need watering far more often than you can manage, so pot them on into bigger pots with much more compost and they'll last longer between waterings. Indeed, the best way to reduce watering frequency is to pot everything into bigger pots or, better still, with ornamentals, put several in an even bigger planter.

With vegetables, and to a lesser extent fruits, one good soaking when you see the flowers appear can double your crop. This is especially true in drier counties when flowers on potatoes, corn, and pulses should be seen as the sign to pour water on really generously.

Always water before the plant wilts! If you leave watering until this point is reached serious damage has occurred and the plant will have suffered a check it will likely never recover from. However, there is a neat trick to help: some plants, such as daturas and phloxes, wilt well before most others, so having these as indicators among other plants will give you an early warning that the danger point is near.

Left: Potatoes grown in tubs under cover need lashings of water or they crop lightly

What to water

Obviously, it's sensible to prioritize watering to those plants that need it most. Small seedlings have shallow roots and must be given moist soil or they never thrive. Plants in small pots need watering more urgently than the same in bigger ones. Hanging baskets are especially vulnerable, as hanging in the air they get the water drawn out of them (like your clothes drying on a line). Recent transplants and those perennials planted in the last six months are all in need of watering more often than well-established ones. In the vegetable garden, the salad and leaf crops become bitter if grown dry and need to be kept perpetually moist. And plants on or against a wall get less rain than those in the open, plus the wall may suck moisture away, so these need extra watering—especially peaches and pears trained against walls.

Left: Set filled watering cans to warm up, ready for next time.

What water to use?

The source of the water makes a difference; rain is best, and clean rainwater from a bucket is warmer than well or pond water, and ditch and dirty water may carry disease. Obviously rain doesn't fall everywhere equally, and that's not only by region but also locally, and rain may almost totally avoid certain spots, like the area behind walls that receive a regular soaking. Large trees, tall hedges, buildings, and other obstacles can also make one part much drier than the rest. One way to find out if this is the case is to stand a dozen tins in different spots and see how they compare after rain. A can placed in the middle of an open lawn will tell you how much has fallen on average, or you can buy a proper rain gauge. Every roof, from the house and garage to garden shed, greenhouse, and dog house, ought to be guttered and the rainwater delivered to cisterns, tanks, or buckets for use later.

Rain does something special, acting a bit like a pump. When you water one area by hand, even heavily, much of the water soaks in sideways and it's hard to apply enough to drench the soil. Rain, however, manages this as it's widespread and thus a heavy fall expels all air from earthworm tunnels, soil fissures, and gaps between particles. Then (unless you have a grievous clay) this soaking drains down, sucking fresh air in after it. Rain is also aerated by its long fall and bouncing about, and so it oxygenates the soil. This is good as most soil organisms and plant roots give off carbon dioxide and need oxygen.

Given the choice, I'd prefer not to use tap water for most watering as it's full of unwanted chlorine (and now fluoride as well), and in my region it's very hard, so excess salts build up in pots and it cannot be used on acid lovers. But, being sterile, tap water, preferably pre-warmed, is best for tiny seedlings, especially tender ones. It's also convenient, useful for fast delivery and, with permission (you pay the water company), can be used for sprinklers and other automatic systems.

Above: A row of plastic bins stores a lot of water, even if not exactly portable
Right: Looks like a proper job but, as with the bins next door, each overflow will erode the standing on the side it runs down. However, there are ways to avoid this

Every roof, from the house and garage to garden shed, greenhouse, and dog house, ought to be guttered and the rainwater delivered to cisterns, tanks, or barrels for use later.

Tapping into Nature's resources

Above: Beware pouring silty mud into pots as it blocks airways

Right: This man-made pool lined with plastic is conveniently near the fruit cage and vegetable beds

As you cannot rely on the rain, try to preserve water in the soil with mulches and by increasing the humus content. Consider increasing natural reserves of water such as ponds and make every effort to store rainwater rather than using the mains tap, as this is beneficial from both environmental and financial perspectives.

If you have a well of your own, you may use the water even during watering bans and in huge quantities. However, although useful it's usually cold, not sterile, and may be limey in most regions. If it's a groundwater well, as opposed to a deep one, it will be even less sterile, possibly even nastily contaminated.

Ponds and ditches are definitely not sterile and are often contaminated with all sorts, but they are not so cold, although hardly warm. They are handy as a source of emergency water or for ornamentals, but their water is not recommended for regular use on food crops because of the risks of contamination.

Unfortunately there is no room in this book to go into the technicalities of gray water recycling, rush beds, and septic tanks, but all of us can reuse the water from our bath, shower, or kitchen sink for watering our gardens with little complication or effort. However, water from washing and dishwashing machines and

that processed by water softeners carries too many chemicals to be recommended. The simplest way to use gray water is to empty it into watering cans and apply it by hand. You might have diverters fitted to waste pipes to take it somewhere convenient, allowing it to run into the ground near trees or shrubs. Such a soak-away method must only be temporary, and you should move the outlet regularly to a new place, covering the old site with a sprinkling of soil to prevent smells. Do not store gray water as it pongs and, technically, becomes a health hazard. For hygiene's sake, do not use gray water on salad and other crops eaten raw, although it's fine for those that are cooked.

The next best thing is to store rainwater, and as much of it as possible! Water barrels are the ideal solution and can be fitted to guttering on sheds, greenhouses, or even the dog house to collect the water as it falls, and you can fit barrels in even the smallest of gardens. Buy bigger barrels as they're cheaper per gallon, and buy more of them, or convert dead chest freezers, oil drums, and whatever. Have many and link them together with hosepipes (see siphons, below) so their overflows fill each other in turn with a proper soak-away at the end. Make sure none of your barrels spill over as this may undermine that side or damage property. On a small scale, 1-gallon clear plastic water bottles are convenient. These can be filled in winter, placed around plants as a warming wall in spring, and later emptied as needed.

One of the greatest labor-saving devices to help move water is a siphon. A piece of hose is run between two barrels, draped over the rims, and hung down to the bottoms, held in place with weights. Fill this hose with water (by a mains hose is easiest, or immerse the whole hose, then lift one end out and take it away to be positioned in the next barrel with the thumb pressed firmly over the end and do not release it until in place). The water will come to the same level in both. If the barrels are on the same level, each will fill up to the brim in rain; but if one is higher or lower than the other it will need dropping in a hole or raising on blocks until the brims, or rather the overflows, are at the same level. Now the advantage this system

Have many water barrels and link them together with hosepipes so their overflows fill each other in turn with a proper soak-away at the end.

has over a simple overflow is that the two barrels will always keep the water in them at the same level; so if one is outside the greenhouse and the other inside, you can draw on the one inside until all the water of both (save a drop in the bottom) has been drawn—without ever walking around to get it. And the two barrels do not have to be near each other, they can be hundreds of yards apart—though the further they are the slower the recharge rate. But, just as importantly again, you can connect as many together as you like; a barrel under each gutter can be connected with a dozen more stood elsewhere, even out of sight. You can add or take from any one, which then adds or draws down from all of them. The brilliance is that you can site a barrel right near the vegetable plot, dahlia bed, patio, or wherever you frequently want to water, then you just keep drawing from it, leave it near empty and come back later and it's full again. Marvelous.

The dark green hose delivers water from a huge outdoor tank, the black hose passes some on to the next barrel where the blue-green hose passes water to yet another barrel

Each time water is used, the barrels refill. If after heavy use with no rain their level falls too much, their support can be removed to lower them

Using good-quality water

Although trials have shown there is only a little advantage to using warm water, I do not believe them. If I were a plant I'd still prefer warm baths and showers to cold ones, no matter if the latter are allegedly more healthy. You can add a little hot water when filling a watering can at a sink, or bring water up to room temperature by filling and standing the watering cans indoors overnight or in the sun some hours before use. Placing a water barrel inside the greenhouse or just in a warm corner and refilling it after every use is another way of getting the same result. It's certainly a bad idea to drench or stand small pots of tender seedlings in ice-cold water.

For sowing and watering small seedlings it's essential that only fresh tap water is used. For some other plants, such as members of the cucurbit family, it's better to use tap water (at least until cropping is well underway), as any water from a dirty source may carry cucumber mosaic virus. You could add a sterilizing chemical to water barrels, but this may itself make the water unsuitable. Several natural "sterilizers" have been tried and the most effective ones seem to be where other beneficial fungi either occupy the niche or neutralize the problem ones. However, using tap water seems the simplest solution. Check the pH level of your tap water, its acid-alkaline value. Most tap water is hard, limey, or slightly alkaline and therefore suitable for most plants in moderation. However, such alkaline water does not suit acid lovers; the ericaceous family, such as heathers, and some others such as citrus and most houseplants. (Most of these are tender, from tropical forests, where the soils are acid, and as they're in a warm dry place they transpire heavily using much water, so slowly the salts build up in a pot until the compost crusts with whitish deposits. That's the time to flush and repot with new compost.) Rainwater is usually acidic and so is best for most plants, preferably as delivered, but even when stored it's still good stuff.

As mentioned before, rain is aerated and so rich in oxygen, whereas most other water has little or none. I half-fill a bottle with suitable water and then shake it vigorously to aerate it for my most important seed and seedlings, however this is not so feasible on a larger scale.

Placing a water barrel inside the greenhouse or just in a warm corner and re-filling it after every use is another way of getting warm water.

How to water

The aim is to wet the compost or soil, making it moist so the plants can take up the water, not to turn it into mud, which will crack and cause fissures, nor to blast bits everywhere, as these cause diseases as well as spoil appearances and are gritty in salads. Pouring water on hastily may just result in it running away, eroding channels as it goes. Watering but occasionally and heavily may be pointless anyway as dry soil or compost are incredibly hard to rewet; they need several attempts to even start moistening them again. Another danger of insufficient watering, especially if badly done regularly, is that plants get used to the top surface being the only wet place so they predominantly root there. If they are not watered at all or the soil is thoroughly soaked and drains well, they will root deeper to find their own water. Thus it's best to water plants in the ground on a regular round, applying water heavily every so often until the soil is soaking, and then abstain. In pots and tubs you have to water far more often, and in the growing season even thrice daily.

Watering by soaking is without doubt the best approach for plants in pots, small tubs, and so on. Rather than watering, probably badly, from above, the container is stood in a tray of (preferably warm) water. The water expels the air as it fills the container, which is allowed to stand for, say, a quarter of an hour or so and no more, then it's carefully removed and stood to drain, when it sucks air in again. Watering by pouring water in from above, however, often passes through the compost leaving dry patches. Less effective than soaking, but more convenient, is giving each pot or tub a saucer underneath it. Fill each saucer with water, stand the pot on it and return after a half hour or so; any water that is left can be poured out, or a dry saucer can be given more and, again, you check it after another half an hour. Other than for plants in the full flush of spring growth, particularly tomatoes, it's near fatal to let plants stand for longer in saucers of water as the roots will invariably drown.

Left: Saucers are dangerous as if left full they can rot roots

Watering by hand

Most watering is done with watering cans. Bigger ones mean less journeys than smaller, and a pair make you better balanced and halve the journeys. But when watering small stuff, a big can may be hard to hold at the right level, so I also have a small one for delicate watering, and then I use the big one for transport and to refill the little one.

One of the frequent errors with watering cans is fitting the rose like a shower head so the water drops down from it, which is incorrect. It should be positioned with the holes uppermost so water comes out and up in tiny little arcs that then fall gently on small seedlings, and so forth.

Now hard to find are Victorian spraying syringes, which are like large bicycle pumps that suck up water and squirt it out, making artificial rain. I find these ingenious and also useful for watering and spraying liquids such as seaweed solution. They aerate the water as well as deliver it and I'm convinced of their value for watering plants, such as citrus.

Rather than try to get water to soak in by each plant in the ground, you can create a shallow watering trench around them individually or in a row, or a raised soil wall with a depression in the middle. Then the water can be delivered quickly to slowly soak in just where it's needed.

Funnels made out of plastic bottles, inverted with their bottoms cut off, and placed in the soil by thirsty plants are another way of delivering a lot of water quickly and having it soak in slowly. Simply fill the bottles with water and leave it to drain directly down to the roots.

When watering with hoses you must, by law, have a non-return valve fitted, and, of course, pay for your water. Obviously you also need a mains tap conveniently placed and do not forget to insulate this against winter frost. A hose delivers faster than you can walk with a can. The problem is that the water comes with some force and thus is best combined with a variable nozzle to reduce it to a spray rather than a jet. Even so, a hose at mains pressure can do a lot of damage to tiny plants. One way round this is to use the hose to fill one watering can while you empty another, the water can be directed into a trench or funnel, or the hose can be connected to a sprinkler so the water is sprayed over an area like rain. (By putting a tin can under the sprinkler you can even measure how much "rain" you are applying.) There are a huge number of different sprinklers that can water different-shaped patterns from circular to rectangular and are pretty cheap. The problem is, though, that they deliver the water to everything in much the same way and without any differentiation—and wetting all the foliage encourages diseases while wetting the soil everywhere, which wastes water to evaporation and chills it down at the same time. Thus watering by hand is finer tuned.

Left: I must repeat—make sure the rose is on the opposite way to a shower head!

Other watering systems

Automatic watering systems can significantly reduce the effort of watering, and be a lifesaver if you're away from your garden for a period of time. Automatic timers, mechanical, or computer-controlled devices or those with moisture detectors in the soil or pots can turn on sprinklers already set in place, including overhead ones under cover for a pre-set time. There are also systems that supply water under pressure from the mains or a header tank through a network of small tubes to adjustable dripping devices that go in each pot or by each plant. The drawback with almost all of these, for the average gardener, is that the time taken to set them up is huge. These are more suited to commercial greenhouses. Where you have the average small greenhouse with a mixture of favorite flowering perennials, tomatoes, a whole load of seedlings of bedding, and vegetables, all being potted on ready for moving out, then it's nigh on impossible to have anything other than the gardener water each properly. The time taken to readjust any automatic system for plants that daily use more or less water is impractical.

A seep hose is an efficient, environmentally-friendly way to water, in that less water is lost by evaporation. The hose is laid by or buried with the roots of plants and has a porous skin or tiny perforations that enable it to weep water when under pressure from the mains or a header tank. It does work and is handy for permanent plantings but is not suited for pots, and so on.

Capillary matting is another good way to reduce the effort needed for regular watering in warm weather, and can keep plants well watered indoors if you are away. This matting is made from a non-degradable, thick cloth, on which you place your pots. By putting one end of the matting (or a small strip cut as a "wick") in a tub of water or with an inverted bottle of water on it, the mat delivers water to the plants while replacing it from the reservoir. The plants must have very good contact at the drainage holes for this to work well, and the matting sadly goes green quickly. If you can't get capillary matting, a rope made of twisted strips of cloth with one end left in a jug of water and the other laid on the top of the soil acts as a wick and will transfer water in the same way. The higher the jug is raised, the faster the water is transferred.

Above: Capillary matting (or an old towel) can keep
your plants watered semi-automatically

Specific watering issues

When watering under cover, one big difference is that the watering will affect the humidity levels around the plants, whereas outdoors it has little impact. Some plants like a degree of humidity at certain times, but generally too much is a problem. This is especially so in autumn and winter as growth slows, for then humid conditions can cause gray molds and rots to proliferate. Be careful when and how you water at these times, do not splash the stuff about except when specifically required, such as in summer when tomatoes or grapes are flowering.

Dried-out plants are a disaster that is hard to recover from. Pots and hanging baskets cannot easily be rewetted by just pouring on water, as it will just run through the soil. Multiple small wettings will work slowly, and adding a drop of detergent and using warm water also works, but much better still is simply immersing them in a bowl of water for half an hour or so almost to the rim. One other trick that works with non-tender plants is placing ice cubes on their compost in hot weather, as these melt slowly, allowing their water to be absorbed.

If a bag of potting compost dries out to a powder before you get round to using it, mix about half of it with water to form a muddy slurry. Then mix in the dry half and leave to stand. This should then be moist but not slippery. It's worth sifting it before use to reintroduce air.

Right: This is a cunning technique—the water in the outer saucer is a moat to stop crawling pests such as vine weevil getting to or from the pot standing in the inner saucer

Feeding

Along with light, water, and air plants need mineral food, most of which they can find if they are in the ground but one of the gardener's jobs is to top up the supplies. Obviously, plants in pots cannot find all they need, so the gardener must supply it. Some plants are hungrier than others and some need different nutrients at different times of their growth cycle, so it's important to know what to do when. Sensible gardeners feed the soil or compost with natural fertility-containing substances, which break down to first feed the soil organisms and then go on to feed the plants (rather than adding concentrated chemical fertilizers which may overwhelm them or wash out and damage the environment). Admittedly, in the end either approach supplies much the same substances but the natural ones are in a safer form. To use an analogy, a glass of wine with each meal is healthy, but concentrate a month's supply into one dose and you're dead.

Left: Radishes need such rich moist soil or they will grow slowly and become fibrous and hot

Why feed?

Plants get up to 90 percent of their raw material as water and most of the rest is carbon dioxide from the air. The tiny fraction left is their input of elements, most of which are minerals dissolved in the soil solution that they take up. (With a microscopic amount of other complex compounds, including antibiotics and vitamins, produced by soil organisms such as the mycorrhizal fungi which live on and in plant roots.) As small as the amounts of these elements and micronutrients are, they're crucial. Indeed, a shortage of any one of these can result in various symptoms of ill health, such as the interveinal yellowing of leaves, poor leaf color, or colored edges, or light crops of low quality—if any. Just a minute deficiency may make plants much more susceptible to pests and diseases, a major shortage and some may not survive long at all. However, an excess of nutrients may be fatal too.

Why not to feed?

Fertilizer can kill if wrongly applied! Excessive fertilizer concentrations of any form—chemical crystals or even manure (especially raw manure or one containing too much urine)—will kill. You can kill most plants with ordinary salt—this was known even in Biblical times. The salt slowly dissolves, sucking in water, and then when it reaches the roots the strong saline solution sucks water out of the roots rather than the roots sucking it up. The salt solution also sucks the moisture out of soil organisms and everything else it touches until well diluted, at which point it becomes available as a minor source of fertility, but by then most things are dead or injured.

Soluble chemical fertilizers, such as those white crystals from a bag, are no different in this way from ordinary salt; although their elements are needed, a surplus is very damaging and will suck the water out of roots and other living things. Of course, such soluble fertilizers when used in moderation are not so pernicious. As a house plant feed, with enough to cover a fingernail dissolved in several pints of water, they're fine. If they were always only used in the same manner, well diluted with water, they would not cause problems, but when distributed as granules, each sucks the life out of all around it until it has dissolved to a great dilution. This detrimental effect of soluble chemical fertilizers is one reason why they're not used by organic gardeners. However, there's also a second reason: using soluble fertilizers, especially those with a high nitrogen content, affects the soil population, even if they do not kill it all off. The extra soluble nitrogen salts reduces the populations of those microorganisms that fix nitrogen from the air as nitrates and who then provided this nutrient to our plants. And, worse, adding soluble nitrogen salts encourages other microorganisms that break these down back to the unabsorbable gaseous nitrogen again. So using excessive chemical fertilizers can quickly destroy the soil's ability to feed the plants naturally.

Right: Rotting borage leaves in water
makes a free liquid feed

Why use organic fertilizers?

Even just a small excess of soluble nitrogen salts in the soil solution can make the plants grow too lushly, too soft, and too plumped up with water, so they get "thirsty" and they become very prone to pests and diseases. Likewise, imbalances of other nutrients can render the soil and then the plants less healthy. Thus, organic gardeners use fertilizers that do not overwhelm the soil or plants and work by releasing their fertility slowly.

Well-rotted manure, composts, rock dusts, and so on, all dissolve slowly, adding nutrients to the soil and the plants a little bit at a time which they can constantly take up. In this way, high concentrations of nutrients, with all their attendant problems, are avoided.

In theory, most soils in the open ground have more than enough of almost all nutrients to sustain plant growth for millennia. However, these are too often present in an insoluble form that the plants can't directly get at. This is where a healthy soil population of microorganisms is so important, especially those symbiotic ones living on plant roots known as mycorrhizals. They "eat" rock and mineral particles, digesting part of them and making this available as waste products that the plants can then take up in exchange for sugars and other substances from the plants. These microorganisms need water and organic materials to help them do this, so although we may give the soil only a tiny amount of instantly available fertility when we add compost, well-rotted manure, or incorporate green manures, these power the little factories that convert raw soil materials into yet more fertility.

When we add, say, a handful of bone dust, this stimulates population explosions of the microlife that can use this as a resource. So they increase in numbers, producing lots of

Right: Compost, manure, and bark mulches suppress weeds, darken soil, conserve moisture, and add to fertility

wastes rich in phosphates from the bones. But they don't live forever; some die and, as they decay, they release the phosphates they have imbibed, along with lots of other nutrients. Many of the bone eaters are themselves eaten by other microorganisms, which in turn have a population explosion with more wastes and decaying bodies. Once more, in turn, these may be predated by a third, fourth, and fifth group of microcritters, and so on. All of these release carbon dioxide into the soil, which helps dissolve more minerals from the rock particles, and on escaping from the soil this gas is absorbed by the plants' leaves, which combine it with sunlight and water. Now, although carbon dioxide is in excess in the upper atmosphere and causes the greenhouse warming effect, down at plant level it is usually in short supply as plants take it up whenever they are in sunlight. The only time carbon dioxide is given off and heads for the upper atmosphere is when the soil is bare with no plants to absorb it, or if they are in the dark or too cold. But, in the last case, the soil is cold as well, so less activity takes place and less carbon dioxide is released. However, bare soil is bad—carbon dioxide is lost and nutrients liberated in the soil are not utilized and leach away. So it is of vital importance to keep the ground covered, even with weeds, or, better, by using green manures (see page 108).

Ultimately, we feed the soil to feed our plants: organic, and traditional, gardeners are in effect tending a microscopic empire and encouraging the proliferation of vast hordes of countless forms of microlife. All of these become fodder for the larger forms, which go on to feed the worms and eventually the birds and other higher animals. And the whole chain continuously excretes wastes and produces decaying bodies to feed our plants with an incredibly rich mixture of nutrients we cannot hope to duplicate with a mere handful of chemicals. We truly feed the soil to feast our plants.

Left: New shoots pushing up through a weed-free mulch will be near maintenance-free and well fed and, if not watered, at least kept moister

Feeding plants in pots

Now, whereas in the open ground a plant can extend its root system further and further to find scarce materials, in a pot, tub, or whatever it cannot, and so is wholly dependent on the gardener supplying these. Although we can sometimes move a plant up to a bigger pot that holds more compost and therefore more nutrients, this is not always practical and will not solve the problem in the long term when even these increased stocks are depleted. So not only must we water plants in pots diligently but, likewise, we must also very carefully provide all the required nutrients. And, as with feeding plants in the open ground, and indeed much more so, we must be careful never to overdose pots with fertilizer or the effects will be disastrous. I suspect more potted plant deaths are caused by over-considerate gardeners overfeeding than are ever caused by insufficient feeding! If in doubt—don't!

As with most things it helps to read the instructions on the packet (of organic or other fertilizer), to feed sparingly, predominantly during the flush of spring growth and not when plants are approaching dormancy in autumn.

Above: Top dressing of slow release organic fertilizers, is scratched into top of compost

Right: Fresh potting compost will keep this supplied with essentials for months, maybe a year or more—but it will always need potting on or feeding sooner or later

Right food for

the right purpose

NPK is the abbreviation for the elements nitrogen, phosphorus, and potassium, long considered the only important minerals for plants. This dominance was probably because they were the ones first discovered and appear in the larger quantities. Still often listed as the only values for a fertilizer, we now know that other elements are just as critical, especially calcium and sulphur and the many others called micronutrients.

However, in practice it is true that a shortage of any of the big three may more often be a problem, and indeed this is not uncommon and in most soils in the United States there are seldom shortages of most other elements, save for calcium, which occurs only in limey soils. Of course, the elements may be present but may not be very accessible to the plants without the liberating soil microlife. Nitrogen is made available to plants from the air by soil organisms, but we can add it in various forms, such as dried blood, hoof and horn meal, and fish emulsion, or less wisely as chemical forms, such as nitrates and ammoniacal salts. Nitrogen is said to be the most important mineral for growth—too little of it and plants stall, are spindly, and poorly colored; too much and they go dark green, soft, lush, and may even die. All plants need nitrogen, though the legumes (pea, bean, and clover family) usually have their own microorganisms on their roots which "make" it for them. Grasses, corn, salad, and other leaf crops respond most to nitrogenous applications.

Phosphorus is found in dung and bone meal and is chemically bound up as phosphates. Phosphorus is very reliant on microlife to keep it in the soil solution, as many of its interactions with other elements leave it insoluble and so relatively unavailable directly to plants. It's said to be most important for root growth, but it has a host of plant uses and a lack of it results in small flavorless crops, especially in strawberries and corn.

Potassium is found especially in wood ashes; chemical fertilizers contain it as various salts, often as the sulphate. Much more soluble in all forms, it's soon leached away by excess watering or heavy rain so it can easily become in short supply. Potassium is important for the overall health and disease resistance of most plants and for the flavor of produce; it is needed most by certain crops, especially cooking apples, gooseberries, tomatoes, potatoes, and onions.

Calcium is needed by many plants, but not by the lime-hating calcifuge ericaceous family, containing plants such as heathers and rhododendrons. Calcium is usually supplied as ground lime rock, which is just chalk. A good dressing every fourth year is necessary to keep the vegetable plot productive, and it is appreciated by most grass swards except the very fine-growing acid-loving varieties. Lime is also good added to compost heaps, enriching them further by capturing gases such as ammonia which would otherwise escape. Sulphur is needed by many plants but is fortunately well provided in most soils and in manures. It gives the tang to brassicas and is associated with plant resistance to fungal diseases.

Micronutrients are legion, and more are uncovered every day. Almost all the elements, including such rarities as molybdenum, boron, and cobalt, all seem necessary but in incredibly tiny amounts. Therefore, using seaweed products every so often supplies sufficient quantities, as seaweeds contain all these elements in correspondingly small amounts. Many complex organic substances benefit, or may even be necessary for, many plants and are well supplied by applying garden compost and well-rotted manures.

Humus, or organic materials that rot down leaving humus, provides the brown fibrous residue that distinguishes good loam and peaty soils and is not so much a fertilizer but a great source of fertility. While some fertilizers, especially the chemical ones, add little or no humus, well-rotted manures, leaf mold, and garden compost add much. Peat, a controversial substance if taken from peat bogs to the detriment of the environment, is actually remarkably resistant to breaking down, and although eventually forming humus it is not a way to add much direct fertility to the soil. However, it does act as a sponge itself, boosting the water-holding capacity, and thus indirectly increasing the fertility of the soil. But being un-PC it cannot be recommended, unless you live in Eire, in which case you're saving it from being burned in a power station to live on in your garden.

Blueberries and cranberries in an old bath fed with a top
dressing of old leaves held down with ericaceous compost

How and

Because of the danger of overdosing, all fertilizers, including organic ones, should only ever be applied in moderation—and the more powerful ones, the more so. Little and often is the key. As noted previously it's just as with wine; a glass with each meal is good for you, but a week's worth together in one go will make you sick, and a month's supply concentrated to one dose will kill you.

Top dressings are fertilizers (often finely powdered mixtures) that are applied to the soil around a plant in the ground or in a pot. They must not be given too generously or touch the living tissue of the plant, so are best raked or stirred in so they are slowly broken down. It's less effective if it's not mixed in and, if left on the top of the soil, it may attract vermin. Top dressings are mostly given in spring to plants that cannot be potted on any more and to perennial plants, though for the latter case a load of muck is more commonly and effectively applied.

Liquid feeds are very diluted mixtures that must be given with great care. They are mostly used for hungry plants that are confined in pots, and occasionally for stimulating a few in the ground, such as the hungry crops corn, spring greens, tomatoes, and potatoes. These feeds are usually given regularly with the watering throughout the first half of the growing season. The importance of dilution cannot be overstated: if in doubt, dilute by more.

Foliar feeds are much the same as liquid feeds, but are given in an even more dilute form and are sprayed or watered over the upper parts of the plant to be absorbed by the foliage. Although very quick to act, these are also inherently risky; the water needs to be clean, the sun must not be bright and there must not be a wind or such sprays may damage the plants' foliage. However, they are fantastic for correcting minor deficiencies and for boosting flagging plants. Most are applied during the growing season as they are not so readily absorbed when

when to feed

the leaves are absent, though some will be absorbed by other parts. Shoots and bark can absorb water and nutrients, but roots and leaves are better at it! As with any fertilizer, do not apply feeds just before the dormant season, as this encourages soft lush growth that can be damaged by frosts.

In spring, when you keep the greenhouse or cold frame all closed up to preserve the heat, plants soon run out of carbon dioxide. In order to enrich the levels of this gas, on hot days you may ventilate by opening doors and windows, but on colder days when all is shut up the plants will run out of carbon dioxide and growth will stop. Putting a fermenting flagon of anything fruity or sugary with some yeast in the greenhouse provides ample gas, or encourage your pets to snooze in there, or in my case, raise chicks under the staging.

Seaweed solution measured and already part diluted being added to a water barrel

Not for drinking but for the gas, so the caps are on loose

What fertility in what

Of course, every fertilizer has different amounts of various nutrients and some may be short of certain elements, so it's better to use most of them in moderation and in turn, rather than stick to the same one all the time and thus inadvertently cause an imbalance. Also remember that because these are generally slower to break down and become available, they are also longer acting and their benefit may extend over several years or more. The more finely divided and mixed in the fertilizer, the quicker it is to act.

Manures

Manures are the traditional source of almost all fertility. With significant amounts of the major nutrients, traces of most others and huge amounts of potential humus, these are supreme. Ideally, manures are as organic as possible and obtained with the animals' bedding, then wetted, stacked, and composted before use. Raw manure, especially from poultry, risks problems and may even kill plants as it is too strong. The most preferable form is cow manure from breeding herds, then from milkers, and finally from fattening stock. Horse is next best, preferably from working ones, though manure from pet ponies is more widely available. Goat, sheep, llama, pet rabbit, hamster, gerbil manure, and so on, are all good stuff though drier and less active. Pig is strong but nasty to handle; chicken and pigeon manure need to be composted with loads of other stuff and well diluted as it is so fierce. Waterfowl dung, though, is cold and wet and more than all the others far better after incorporating in the compost heap. Worm manure and casts collected from lawns are very rich in all sorts of nutrients and animal by-products and are seriously good stuff. They can best be blended into potting composts or used as top dressings (The solid produce of wormeries is concentrated casts and much like animal manure, the liquid run off is like a liquid feed needing dilution.) Snail droppings are drier and have a higher fiber content, but they are also rich in fertility. Dog, cat, and human manure are actually valuable and used in many parts of the world, but because of laws and matters of public taste, we'd best not go there.

Rather than buying manure and stacking it yourself, you can buy ready-composted manures. These are expensive by comparison, but still good stuff, and as dried out they are better value than they seem. Sewage sludge is similar; rich in phosphates but with some dubious other things included and so are better confined to ornamental areas. Composted bark, if finely ground, is a good mulch and has considerable humus and some nutrients, but is slow to break down and so rarely used for its fertility value. Mushroom compost is widely available and has a lesser but similar fertility value to well-rotted horse manure, and usually it also has some lime. Again, it is rarely employed for fertility, but more for its usefulness as a mulch.

Compost

Garden compost is made from a huge variety of raw materials and so is very good for improving soil fertility. Similar to well-rotted manure, it breaks down to feed the soil and the plants. Many other fertilizers, such as rock dusts (see page 104), are best incorporated in a compost heap, as it makes them more active, and then spread with the compost rather than just added to the soil directly.

Now becoming widely and cheaply available is council compost, which is made from anything that can go through their sifting and selection process, so again this is best on ornamentals, not edibles. It has a variable range of fertility but is comparable with garden compost.

Garden compost is not just a feed, but an inoculant

Dressings of compost or well-rotted manure enrich but also darken and so warm the soil

Animal products

Animal products are also available, such as dried blood which is very rich in nitrogen and is quick acting, though not nice to handle as it smells and taints. Hoof and horn meal is another high-nitrogen source but much slower to act. Fish meal and fish emulsion have significant nitrogen and phosphorus content and almost everything else, so these are wonder feeds but are also expensive and attract vermin and cats. Bone meal is rich in phosphorus and calcium and needed by almost every plant, but it is attractive to vermin and especially to foxes. It is expensive to buy, so collect bones whenever possible, burn them on a small bonfire, and then powder the baked bones with the ashes. Fish, blood, and bone meal is a commercial blend that gives a well-balanced, general-purpose fertilizer for most plants. Guano, petrified seagull droppings, are singularly effective and are very rich sources of nitrogen and potassium, but they are so strong and their collection so ecologically unacceptable that they are no longer recommended to organic gardeners. Urine is sterile, rich in nitrogenous compounds, and contains some potassium and phosphorus; it is good once diluted as a liquid feed, though more acceptable combined in the compost heap. It is best fresh as, once stale, the ammonia it gives off is nasty to roots. If you wish to keep it sweeter, add sugar—honest, this works!

Looks innocuous, not very nice stuff this, but very effective

Soy and seaweed

Soybean meal and corn starch are also occasionally used as fertilizers, as is waste milk and fermentation by-products, but they have little general use and are probably best added to the compost heap.

Seaweed products are especially valuable for their wide range of elements and some should be applied at least once a year. Seaweed meal is excellent and has some nitrogen, as well as saponin soap-like compounds that help gel the soil particles. Calcified seaweed is more like a lime or chalk but with all the extra trace elements as well. It is also said to stimulate microlife, who like its holey texture, and it is the best form of lime to add to compost heaps. Seaweed solution is my favorite, containing all the trace elements, and is a vitamin tonic rather than a feed. I spray it on everything, myself included, once a month from bud burst to leaf fall. It is always applied well diluted and usually as a foliar feed but it is also sometimes watered on. Plants given it regularly definitely become healthier and more resistant to pests and disease.

Seaweed solution is never watered on stronger than this dilution (small container on top of watering can, diluted in full can) and sprayed on as a foliar feed diluted by twice as much again

Seaweed solution is my favorite, containing all the trace elements, and is a vitamin tonic rather than a feed.

Dust, ash, and soot

Rock dusts can be applied to the soil and raked in or passed through the compost heap to make them more active. The most common is lime, which is chalk and mostly calcium carbonate, though the Dolomitic form also has additional magnesium. It is available finely ground and is especially needed every fourth year on vegetable beds, for pitted fruits and for keeping compost sweet. Ground rock potash, high in potassium, and ground rock phosphate, high in phosphorus, are similar dusts and are also available, but not widely. Granite, basalt, and other finely ground tailings from quarries are considered by some to be miracle fertilizers. They are of most use on old worked-out soils, especially the sandy ones that are low in clay. Again, they are better activated by being passed through a compost heap. A few dollops of clay dissolved to a fine slurry and splattered about with a big brush is another similar rich source of finely divided minerals, and it is much cheaper than rock dusts.

Other fertilizers include wood ashes; those made from prunings and bonfires are better than those from wood fires, while coal ashes are of little value. Wood ashes contain most elements and are especially rich in potassium, but they may also have much calcium and should be used with care near acid lovers. They need to be collected and kept dry; they are quite caustic and quick acting so they should be given during the growing season; in winter they may just leach away.

Soot is now considered a fertilizer of dubious value as it may contain dioxins and other dangerous combustion products or residues. It certainly should not be used from fires burning anything other than clean fuels. It has some nitrogenous value, many trace elements, and the black carbon part darkens and so warms soils. The old boys reckoned soot water was *the* feed for pineapples and citrus.

Right: A top dressing with plenty of lime for a potted apricot

Finely ground cocoa shell is the powdery form of the shells that is sold as a slug-repellent mulch. Very rich in nitrogen for a plant product, they are used in vegetarian feed mixes in place of dried blood and hoof and horn meal. They need to be mixed in, as they soon turn to a green cardboard once wetted.

Sequestrated products are soluble combinations of iron that keep it available even in limey conditions. These allow acid-loving plants to survive in unsuitable conditions, so it's more a medicine than a fertilizer. Sequestrated products are not recommended for organic gardeners as they are considered too artificial a product.

Epsom salts, magnesium sulphate, is hardly a feed and also more of a medicine, but as it supplies magnesium it is useful in cases of obvious shortage, though not recommended to organic gardeners as it is too strong.

Plant teas are also useful. Rotted-down comfrey leaves, once diluted in water to a very pale solution, make an excellent high-potash feed that is especially good for tomatoes. However, this is a bit high for many other plants, so mix in borage leaves, which have more magnesium and stinging nettles for silica and iron. Straight stinging nettle tea is more of a tonic than a feed, as are other herb teas. Equisetum tea is good for plants for its high silica content that provides silicon, which is important for plant cell walls. Many plants are grown most successfully when fed with well-diluted borage tea, too.

Left: Not an over-generous top dressing but a mulch of sharp sand covering one

Green manures

Green manures are crops of plants sown and grown in spare soil, such as over winter, that are rotted down for their fertility value either in situ or through the compost heap. (They are most effectively incorporated by covering them with a black plastic, light-excluding sheet in late winter, and then a couple of months later they have disappeared into the soil, leaving it richer and in good tilth.) It is important to dig these plants in or compost them before flowering and setting seed, as then the nutrients would become locked up in the seeds, and because as the plants mature they get more fibrous and harder to incorporate. Thus several short crops are better than one left longer. Most of those commonly on offer are hard to dig in, hard to take away, and recover viciously, thus they are more suited to farms with huge tractors and plows and not to gardens. I strongly recommend green manure seeds such as Hungarian grazing rye; tares, vetches, and clovers are only employed if you are really good at weed control. Otherwise I suggest you use easier to deal with plants such as borage, mustard, poached egg plant (*Limnanthes douglasii*), lamb's lettuce (*Valerianella*), and miner's lettuce (*Claytonia/Montia perfoliata*). The legumes, peas, and beans, and clovers, lupins, and others are all especially good at fixing nitrogen, so they all make good green manures if dug in while young. Some plants are especially good at accumulating certain elements. For example, melons have high levels of calcium in their leaves and daturas accumulate phosphates. Growing green manures of these scavenges the soil for these minerals, concentrates them in the plants, which are then composted or dug in to release their acquired wealth for following plants.

Rather annoyingly, the best plants for mineral accumulation and ground covering green manuring are usually weeds—but that's another book.

Left: Lamb's lettuce, *Valerianella*, makes a good salad and a green manure if left
Right: Comfrey produces masses of succulent leaves to enrich your compost

And one final word—with everything you do, think it through at least three times, measure at least twice, then do it but once and properly!

Index

animal products 102, 107
anti-capping 41
ash 104
automatic watering systems 78

bare-root plants 48, 56-7
bark, composted 100
blood, dried 102
bone meal 102
bones 86-9, 102
bulbs 50-2

calcium 93, 94, 102, 104
capillary matting 78
chitting 20
cloches 41
cocoa shell 107
composts 24, 28, 38, 39, 75, 80, 83, 86, 100, 101
corn starch 103

damping off 31
diseases and pests 14, 31, 34, 38, 56
dividing plants 48
drainage 24

feeding 6, 45, 83-5
    how and when 96-7
    organic fertilizers 86-9
    plants in pots 90
    right food 93-4
fertilizers 84-5, 86-9, 96, 98-108
fish meal 102
foliar feeds 96-7
frost 41, 45, 77

germination 12, 28-9, 31
green manures 86, 108
gray water 68-70

hanging baskets 65, 80
hardening off 32-3, 44
hoses 66, 77, 78
humidity 80
humus 94

John Innes sowing compost 24, 28

laying seed on edge 20

life span of seeds 18
light 14, 32
lime 94, 104
liquid feeds 96

magnesium sulphate 107
manures 86, 100
micro-life 93 103
micronutrients 93-4
minerals 93-4
mulches 49, 51, 68, 100, 107
mushroom compost 100
mycorrhiza 86

nitrogen 93, 102, 107

organic fertilizers 86-9

paper tapes 20
peat 94
pests and diseases 34, 38, 41, 45, 49, 84, 86
phosphorus 93, 102, 104
plant teas 107
planting 6, 42-5
    bulbs, corms, and rhizomes 50-2
    planting holes 44-5
    soft, small, and herbaceous plants 46-9
    trees and shrubs 55-7
potassium 93, 94, 102, 104
pots 22, 65, 80, 83, 90
potting on 34-7
pre-germination of seeds 20
pre-soaking seeds 20
preparation for sowing 24-9
pricking out 34-7
propagators 32

rainwater 31, 66, 67, 70, 72
rock dusts 86, 100, 104

scorch 14, 32
seaweed 94, 103
seed 9-11, 12, 18-20
seedlings 9, 14, 31, 42, 65, 72
    growing conditions 32-3
    pricking out and potting on

34-7
seep hoses 78
sequestrated products 107
shrubs 44, 55-7
sieving 28, 80
soaking 75
soil 6, 38, 79, 83, 86, 89
    pre-warming soil 39
soot 104
sowing 6, 9, 42
    outdoors 38-41
    preparation 24-9
    sow sparingly 17, 22
    under cover 22
soy 103
storage of seeds 18
stratifying seeds 14, 18
sulphur 93, 94
supports 34, 55-6

tap water 31, 66, 72
temperature 14
testing seeds 18
top dressings 96
transpiration 60, 61
trees 44, 55-7

urine 102

vernalizing seeds 18

warmth 14, 22, 32, 39, 41
watering 6, 45, 55, 58-61
    before sowing 39
    good-quality water 72
    how to water 75
    nature's resources 68-71
    specific issues 80
    watering by hand 76-7
    watering systems 78
    what to water 65
    what water to use 66-7
    when to water 62-3
weeding 45, 55
wilting 63